www.futuresmartminds.com

Welcome to the **FutureSmartMinds** family!

Thank you for choosing "**Future Chef**" as your culinary adventure guide. We're thrilled to have you on board as we embark on a journey to develop the talents of young minds in STEM (Science, Technology, Engineering, and Mathematics) fields. Your support means the world to us. By investing in "**Future Chef**," you're not only inspiring young chefs but also empowering the future generation with invaluable STEM skills.

we kindly invite you to share your thoughts about "**Future Chef**" on Amazon. Your feedback helps us continue to improve and inspire more young minds. Your honest review will guide others in making their choice and encourage them to join us in shaping the future of our future smart minds.

Scan to Rate Us on Amazon

Once again, thank you for being a part of our FutureSmartMinds community. We're excited to have you with us on this journey.

Warm regards,

The **FutureSmartMinds** Team

www.futuresmartminds.com

Email: FutureSmartMindsKids@gmail.com

 @futuresmartminds

 @futuresmartminds

 @ futuresmartminds

Scan to visit our website

 1

Content	Page
Cooking Science	4

Bake

Grill

Cooking Science

When you step into the kitchen to cook, you become a scientist, even if you don't realize it. You're like a scientist mixing different chemicals (ingredients) when you cook. For example, when you make a cake, you combine flour, eggs, sugar, and more. Each ingredient plays a specific role, just like chemicals in a science experiment.

Cooking involves different scientific processes, such as Chemical Reactions, Heat Transfer, State Changes, Taste of Senses, and Time and Precision. Let's break down how **cooking** and **science** are connected:

Ingredients

Imagine your kitchen as a laboratory where your ingredients are your chemicals. Each ingredient has a specific role in your recipe, just like each chemical's role in a reaction. For example, when you bake a cake, you use flour, egg, and baking powder.

➢ **Flour** gives a structure to your cake. It is like the foundation of a building.
➢ **Eggs** help mix your ingredients. It is like bonding between atoms that make molecules.
➢ **Baking powder** allows your cake to rise and become fluffy. It is like gases which expand and fill the space.
➢ **Heat** is the magic wand that changes raw ingredients into a tasty cake.

Changing States

In cooking, states change between solids, liquids, and gases. For example, water (a liquid) boils and turns into steam (a gas). When you freeze juice (a liquid), it becomes an ice pop (a solid). Cooking shows you the science of changing states in action.

➢ **Melting:** when you melt cheese, it transforms from solid into liquid. This is like how ice melts into water, changing states from solid to liquid.
➢ **Boiling:** when you boil water, it changes from liquid to gas. Boiling is an essential scientific process used in many applications around you.

Chemical Reactions

When ingredients come together, they create chemical reactions. This is like mixing different chemicals in a lab, but it's tastier!

Yeast in Bread: Yeast is a tiny living thing. When you mix yeast with warm water and sugar, it starts to eat the sugar. As it eats, it releases gas. This gas makes the dough puff up. That's why bread rises and becomes soft and fluffy.

Caramelization: When you heat sugar, like when making caramel or roasting marshmallows, the sugar changes color and becomes a sweet syrup. This change is a chemical reaction.

Taste and Senses

In science, we use our senses to observe and understand things. Cooking is similar. You see how food changes color while cooking (sight sense). You smell delicious aromas (smell sense). You taste different flavors (taste sense).

It's all about using your senses to explore and learn. Cooking starts with choosing the right ingredients. You'll use ingredients like sugar and chocolate to make a sweet dessert.

You might use spices, meat, and veggies for a lovely meal. The ingredients you choose affect the taste of your dish. The way you cook also matters; frying something can become crispy and delicious, whereas boiling makes things tender, and grilling can give a smoky flavor. The way you cook impacts how your food tastes. Adding salt, pepper, herbs, and spices enhances the flavor of your dish. Seasoning can make your food taste better and more enjoyable.

Taste Buds: When you eat, your taste buds come into play. You have taste buds on your tongue, and they can detect different flavors: sweet, salty, sour, and bitter. The combination of these flavors creates the taste of what you're eating.

Smell: Your sense of smell is connected to your sense of taste. When you smell food, your taste buds get excited. Smelling food give you a hint of what it might taste like.

Texture: The texture of food matters, too. Something crispy or crunchy feels different in your mouth than something soft or smooth. Texture affects your overall food experience.

Presentation: How food looks on the plate can also influence how it tastes to you. A beautifully presented dish can make it more appealing and tastier.

Sound: Even the sound of food can affect your perception of taste. For example, the sizzle of food in a hot pan can make it seem more appetizing.

Creativity

Scientists use their creativity to discover new things. In the kitchen, you're a scientist creating edible art. You can follow recipes as if they're instructions, just like scientists do with experiments. You can also be creative. Think of it as creating your own experiments with flavors, and your kitchen is your laboratory.

So, when you're cooking, you're not just making a meal; you're also a scientist exploring, experimenting, and learning along the way. Plus, you get to eat your delicious discoveries!

Unique Combinations: Being creative in the kitchen means trying out unique combinations. You can mix sweet and salty, crunchy and smooth, or even create your own recipes.

Problem Solving: Sometimes, you might run into challenges while cooking. This is where creativity comes into play. You can think of creative solutions to make your dish turn out just right.

Personal Touch: Cooking lets you put your personal touch on everything you make. It's a way to express yourself and share your love and creativity with others.

(1) Fluffy Pancake Alchemy

Making pancakes isn't just about cooking; it's a science-packed baking adventure. It involves mixing ingredients, changing state, and heat transfer processes. Plus, you can eat your unique creation at the end! In this fun baking experiment, you will whip up a batch of pancake batter, sizzle it on a hot grill, and watch the ingredients transform into fluffy, golden pancakes.

Ingredients

- 1 cup all-purpose flour
- 2 tablespoons sugar
- 1 teaspoon baking powder
- 1/2 teaspoon baking soda
- 1/4 teaspoon salt
- 1 cup buttermilk (or mix 1 cup of milk with 1 tablespoon of vinegar and let it sit for a few minutes)
- 1 egg
- 2 tablespoons melted butter
- Butter or oil for cooking
- Optional toppings: syrup, fruit, chocolate chips, or whipped cream

Instructions

(1) Mixing the dry ingredients

In a bowl, mix the flour, sugar, baking powder, baking soda, and salt. This is like gathering your experiment materials.

(2) Mixing the wet ingredients

In another bowl, whisk together the buttermilk, egg, and melted butter. This is like your special liquid solution for your pancake experiment.

(3) Combining dry and wet

Now, mix the dry and wet ingredients together. Stir until you have a smooth batter.

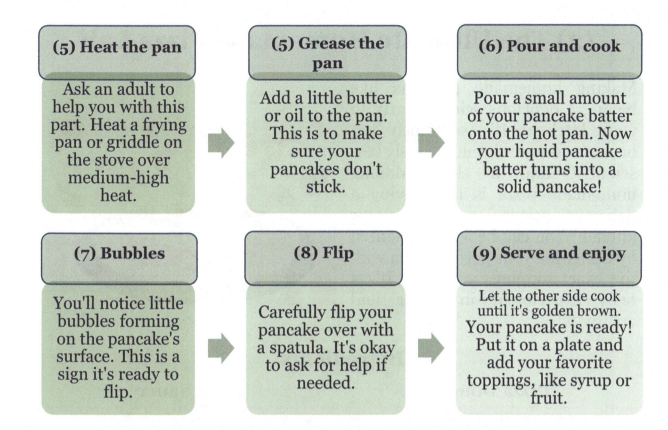

(5) Heat the pan

Ask an adult to help you with this part. Heat a frying pan or griddle on the stove over medium-high heat.

(5) Grease the pan

Add a little butter or oil to the pan. This is to make sure your pancakes don't stick.

(6) Pour and cook

Pour a small amount of your pancake batter onto the hot pan. Now your liquid pancake batter turns into a solid pancake!

(7) Bubbles

You'll notice little bubbles forming on the pancake's surface. This is a sign it's ready to flip.

(8) Flip

Carefully flip your pancake over with a spatula. It's okay to ask for help if needed.

(9) Serve and enjoy

Let the other side cook until it's golden brown. Your pancake is ready! Put it on a plate and add your favorite toppings, like syrup or fruit.

The sizzling science behind fluffy pancake

Chemical reaction: When you mix the pancake batter, you create a chemical reaction between the dry ingredients (flour, baking powder, and sugar) and the wet ones (buttermilk, eggs, and melted butter). Due to the addition of baking powder, these ingredients combine to create tiny gas bubbles. When you cook the batter on a hot grill, the heat causes those bubbles to expand, making your pancakes rise and become fluffy.

Heat: As the pancake cooks, the heat from the grill makes the batter change. It goes from a gooey liquid into a solid pancake since the proteins in the eggs and flour strengthen and hold everything together.

Browning: The browning of your pancakes results from a process called the Maillard reaction, where sugars and amino acids in the batter interact due to the heat, producing those delicious golden-brown colors.

(2) The Ultimate Homemade Pizza Lab

Making homemade pizza is like having a delicious science party in your kitchen! It's so much fun because you can simultaneously be a scientist and a chef. Making homemade pizza is like having a delicious science party in your kitchen! You can be a food scientist by designing your perfect pizza with the exact toppings you love. It's a tasty experiment in flavor and creativity!

Ingredients

Pizza Dough

- 1 packet (2 1/4 tsp) of active dry yeast
- 1 cup warm water (about 110°F or 43°C)
- 1 tsp sugar
- 2 1/2 cups all-purpose flour
- 1 tsp salt
- 2 tbsp olive oil

(you can skip these ingredients if you get pre-prepared Pizza dough.)

Pizza Sauce

- 1 can (14 oz) of crushed tomatoes
- 1 tsp olive oil
- 1 tsp dried oregano
- 1/2 tsp garlic powder
- Salt and pepper
- Toppings (Get creative with your favorite toppings like pepperoni, bell peppers, mushrooms, and more!)

Instructions

The instructions for preparing your homemade pizza consist of 3 parts:

A. Preparing your Pizza dough – *you may skip this part if you get pre-prepared Pizza dough.*

B. Preparing the Pizza sauce.

C. Assembling your Pizza.

A. Preparing your Pizza dough

(1) Activate the yeast

In a small bowl, mix the warm water and sugar. Sprinkle the yeast on top. Let it sit for about 5-10 minutes until it's frothy. The yeast wakes up and starts creating bubbles.

(2) Mix the dry ingredients

In a large bowl, combine the flour and salt.

(3) Combine wet and dry

Pour the yeast mixture and olive oil into the dry ingredients.

(4) Mixing the dough

Mix everything together with your hands to form a dough.

(5) Kneading the dough

Place the dough on a floured surface and knead it for about 5-7 minutes. Kneading is like a mini workout for the dough.

(6) Let the dough rise

Put the dough in a greased bowl, cover it with a kitchen towel, and let it rise for 1-1.5 hours. During this time, the yeast is producing gas bubbles, making the dough rise.

B. Preparing the Pizza sauce

(7) Heat the sauce

Heat the olive oil in a pan and add the crushed tomatoes, oregano, garlic powder, salt, and pepper.

(8) Cook the sauce

Cook for about 10 minutes until the sauce thickens. You're turning the tomatoes into yummy sauce!

C. Assembling your Pizza

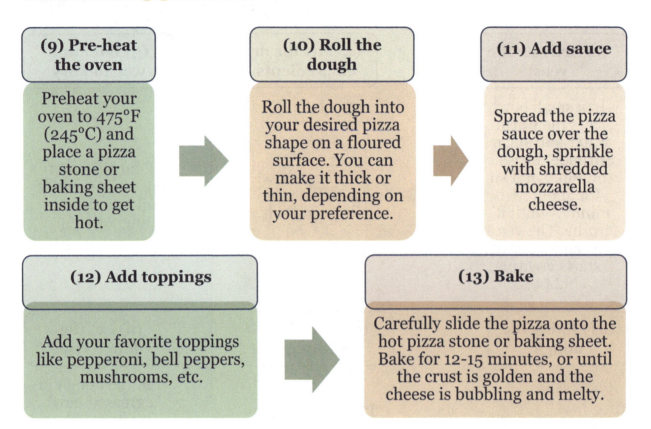

(9) Pre-heat the oven

Preheat your oven to 475°F (245°C) and place a pizza stone or baking sheet inside to get hot.

(10) Roll the dough

Roll the dough into your desired pizza shape on a floured surface. You can make it thick or thin, depending on your preference.

(11) Add sauce

Spread the pizza sauce over the dough, sprinkle with shredded mozzarella cheese.

(12) Add toppings

Add your favorite toppings like pepperoni, bell peppers, mushrooms, etc.

(13) Bake

Carefully slide the pizza onto the hot pizza stone or baking sheet. Bake for 12-15 minutes, or until the crust is golden and the cheese is bubbling and melty.

The sizzling science behind homemade pizza

Yeast Magic: It all starts with the pizza dough. You use a special ingredient called yeast. Yeast is like a tiny living creature, too small to see. When we mix yeast with warm water and some sugar, it gets excited and starts eating the sugar. As it eats, it releases a gas called carbon dioxide. The gas bubbles get trapped in the dough, and that's what makes the dough rise and become all fluffy and airy.

The Oven's Heat: When we preheat the oven, it gets hot, around 475°F (245°C). The heat makes the dough cook when we put our pizza in the oven. The dough has a lot of water, and as it gets super hot, the water turns into steam. The steam helps puff the dough even more, giving you a nice, crispy crust.

Melting Cheese: The cheese on the pizza loves the heat, too. It melts because of the high temperature in the oven. Like ice turns into water when it gets warm, cheese goes from solid to gooey, melty liquid when it gets hot.

Toppings: The toppings on the pizza, like pepperoni, veggies, or whatever you add, cook because of the oven's heat. Some toppings, like pepperoni, release yummy oils as they cook, adding even more flavor.

Explore

1. Explore Different Amounts of Yeast

Make two batches of pizza dough using the same ingredients but varying the amount of yeast in each. Use one with more yeast and one with less. You will notice that the dough with more yeast will rise faster and be puffier, while the one with less yeast will rise more slowly.

2. Explore Different Oven Temperature

Bake two pizzas at different temperatures. A higher temperature (e.g., 475°F) will cook the pizza faster, resulting in a crispier crust, while a lower temperature (e.g., 375°F) will cook it more slowly, creating a softer crust.

3. Explore Different Toppings

Prepare two pizzas with the same dough and sauce but different toppings. For one, use fresh vegetables; for the other, use pre-cooked vegetables. Explore how cooking time affects the texture and taste of toppings.

4. Explore Gluten-Free Dough

Try making a gluten-free pizza dough using alternative flour like almond or rice flour. Explore why the gluten-free dough won't rise like traditional dough.

5. Explore Sauce Variations

Experiment with different tomato sauce types, such as marinara, barbecue, and pesto. Explore how variations in the sauce can change the overall flavor and how heat affects the sauces.

(3) The Sweet Cookie Magic

Bake

Baking cookies isn't just about satisfying your sweet tooth; it's about having a tasty time while learning some yummy science along the way! You can experiment with different ingredients, like adding chocolate chips or nuts, to see how they affect the taste and texture. So, not only do you get to enjoy tasty cookies, but you also get to be a kitchen scientist discovering the magic of baking!

Ingredients

- 1 cup (2 sticks) of butter
- 1 cup of granulated sugar
- 2 large eggs
- 2 teaspoons of vanilla extract
- 2 1/4 cups of all-purpose flour
- 1/2 teaspoon of baking soda
- 1 teaspoon of salt
- 2 cups of chocolate chips

Instructions

(1) Prepare	**(2) Mix**	**(3) Add eggs and vanilla**
Preheat your oven to 350°F (180°C) and line a baking sheet with parchment paper.	In a large bowl, mix the softened butter and sugar together until it's creamy and well combined. This step is essential to ensure your cookies are soft and chewy.	Add the eggs one at a time, mixing well after each. Then, stir in the vanilla extract.

(4) Sift and combine dry

In a separate bowl, sift together the flour, baking soda, and salt. Gradually add the dry mixture to your wet ingredients, stirring until you have cookie dough.

(5) Add chocolate chips

Gently fold in the chocolate chips. You can also get creative by adding nuts or other mix-ins.

(6) Form cookie dough balls

Use a spoon to scoop up bits of dough and roll them into balls. Place them on the prepared baking sheet, leaving some space in between.

(7) Bake

Pop the cookie sheet into the oven and bake for about 10-12 minutes or until the edges turn golden brown. The middle may look slightly undercooked, but that's okay. It'll keep cooking as it cools.

(8) Cool and enjoy

Take the cookies out of the oven and let them cool for a few minutes on the baking sheet. Then, transfer them to a wire rack to cool completely.

The sizzling science behind homemade cookies

Butter and Sugar: mixing the butter and sugar together creates tiny air pockets in the dough. When you bake the cookies, these pockets fill with steam, making your cookies soft and chewy.

Baking Soda: Baking soda helps the cookies rise and spread. It reacts with the other ingredients, releasing carbon dioxide gas that makes the cookies puff up.

Eggs: Eggs provide structure and moisture to the cookies, helping them hold their shape and stay moist.

Chocolate Chips: As the cookies bake, the chocolate chips melt and then re-solidify, creating gooey pockets of chocolate inside your cookies.

(4) The Secrets of Cheese Pie Chemistry

Cooking a cheese pie at home is more than just making a delicious treat; it's also an exciting science experiment! As you mix, knead, and bake, you discover the wonders of chemistry and physics in the kitchen. Understanding these scientific processes can help you become a better chef, and who knows, you might even invent a unique pie recipe of your own someday! So, put on your apron, gather your ingredients, and start a tasty journey through cheese pie science.

Ingredients

- 1 1/4 cups of all-purpose flour
- 1/2 cup of butter (cold and cubed)
- 1/4 cup of ice water
- 3 large eggs
- 2 cups of grated cheese (choose your favorite type)
- 1 cup of milk
- Salt and pepper

Instructions

A. Prepare Your Cheese Pie Dough

1. In a mixing bowl, combine the flour and cold, cubed butter.

2. Use a pastry cutter or your fingers to break down the butter into the flour. This creates a crumbly texture.

3. Slowly add the ice water and knead the mixture until it forms a smooth dough.

4. Wrap the dough in plastic wrap and refrigerate for 30 minutes.

B. Prepare Your Filling

5. In another bowl, whisk the eggs and milk together.

6. Add the grated cheese and season with salt and pepper. Mix well.

C. Assemble Your Pie

7. Preheat your oven to 375°F (190°C).

8. Roll out the chilled dough on a floured surface to fit your pie dish.

9. Place the dough in the pie dish, trimming any excess.

D. Bake and Enjoy!

10. Pour the cheese and egg filling into the pie crust.

11. Bake for about 30-35 minutes or until the filling is set, and the top is golden brown.

12. Let the pie cool for a bit, then slice it and enjoy your homemade cheese pie!

The sizzling science behind homemade cheese pie

Mixing: When you combine the cold butter with the flour, you create a crumbly texture by breaking the fat into tiny pieces. This will result in a flaky crust after baking.

Refrigerating: Refrigerating the dough allows the gluten in the flour to relax, making the crust tender and not tough.

Baking: As the pie bakes, the eggs and milk in the filling create a custard-like texture through a process called coagulation. The heat causes the proteins in the eggs to bond, transforming the liquid into a solid, creamy filling.

Melting: The cheese not only adds flavor but also contributes to the consistency of the filling as it melts and integrates with the custard.

(5) Baking a Spectrum Cake

Bake

Cooking a homemade colorful, layered cake is a delicious treat and a fantastic science experiment. By creating layers with different colors, you're experimenting with density, understanding how substances with varying weights can stack on top of each other. It's like building a tasty rainbow! Have fun experimenting and indulging in your colorful creations!

Ingredients

- 2 1/2 cups all-purpose flour
- 2 1/2 tsp baking powder
- 1/2 tsp salt
- 1 1/2 cups granulated sugar
- 1/2 cup unsalted butter (softened)
- 3 large eggs
- 1 tbsp vanilla extract
- 1 1/4 cups whole milk
- Gel food coloring (various colors)
- 1 batch of buttercream frosting

Instructions

(1) Mixing the dry ingredients

In a large bowl, mix the dry ingredients – flour, baking powder, and salt. This step is like combining different building blocks before you start building your cake.

(2) Creaming butter and sugar

In another bowl, cream the softened butter and sugar. This process is like making the foundation of a cake building by mixing solid and sweet elements.

(3) Adding eggs and vanilla

Next, add the eggs one by one and the vanilla extract. Think of this step as adding key ingredients to make the cake batter stick together like glue.

(4) Mixing the dry and wet ingredients

Now, Gradually add the dry ingredients to the wet ingredients, alternating with the milk, beginning and ending with the dry ingredients. Mix until just combined.

(5) Dividing the batter

Divide the batter into separate bowls, one for each color of the rainbow. Each bowl represents a different layer in your cake.

(6) Adding colors

Add gel food coloring to each bowl. Experiment with mixing primary colors to create secondary colors. This step is like an artist mixing paints to create unique colors.

(7) Baking the layers

Pour each colored batter into greased and floured cake pans. Bake for 20-25 minutes, or until a toothpick inserted into the center comes out clean. Let them cool in the pans for 10 minutes, then transfer them to a wire rack to cool completely.

(8) Layering and frosting

Assemble your layers and use buttercream frosting between them. Think of this step like constructing a colorful building with different floors, each separated by a sweet filling.

The colorful science behind the homemade layered cake

Mixing Colors: We know that there are primary colors, which are red, blue, and yellow. These colors can't be made by mixing other colors. When we combine these primary colors, we create secondary colors. For instance, mixing red and blue makes purple, blue and yellow makes green, and red and yellow makes orange. This color-mixing science is called color theory.

Baking the Cake: We deal with chemistry when baking the cake layers. In the cake batter, there's something called baking powder. Baking powder contains two different substances that are a bit like secret ingredients. When these ingredients get wet and heated in the oven, they react. This reaction releases tiny bubbles of carbon dioxide gas. These bubbles get trapped in the batter, puffing up and turning into a soft and fluffy cake.

Science Unleashed

The Magic of Baking Explained

Baking is a beautiful blend of chemistry and physics. So, the next time you're in the kitchen, remember that you're not just cooking; you're doing delicious science experiments! When you mix ingredients, they react chemically to create delicious compounds and flavors. The dough rises as heat forces gas bubbles to expand, while proteins in flour create structure, determining the texture of your baked goods.

The Rising Magic

When you add ingredients like yeast or baking powder to your dough, you're setting the stage for some rising action. Yeast is like a tiny, single-celled living organism that eats the sugars in your dough and releases carbon dioxide gas (CO_2) through a process called **fermentation**.

Those gas bubbles get trapped in the dough, making it rise and become fluffy. When you bake the dough, the heat causes the yeast to become less active and eventually die. The heat also causes the CO_2 gas bubbles to expand further, raising the bread or cake even more.

On the other hand, baking powder is a chemical leavening agent. It contains an acid (usually cream of tartar) and a base (usually baking soda). A **chemical reaction** begins when you mix baking powder with wet ingredients, such as milk or water, and add it to the dry ingredients. The acid and base in the baking powder react to produce carbon dioxide gas. This gas forms bubbles in the batter or dough. The gas bubbles expand as the batter or dough is exposed to heat during baking.

The Heating Magic

When you place your baking dish in the oven, the process starts with **conduction and convection heat transfer processes. Conduction** is the transfer of heat through direct contact. The air in the oven is heated by electric or gas elements, and this heat is applied to your food through the baking dish. **Convection**, on the other hand, involves the circulation of hot air within the oven. This helps distribute the heat evenly, ensuring that your food bakes uniformly.

As your food heats up, its water content starts to **evaporate**. This is particularly important in baking, as it can affect the texture of your baked goods. For example, in bread, the evaporation of water from the dough increases gas bubbles, making the bread rise. The heat causes the starch granules in flour to absorb water and swell. This process is called **gelatinization** and is crucial for the structure and texture of baked goods.

The Cooling Magic

After baking, the food inside the oven is hot, often reaching high temperatures. When you remove it from the oven, the cooling process begins. Cooling involves the **transfer of heat** from the hot baked item to its surroundings, which are at a lower temperature. The hot food loses heat energy to the cooler air around it, and this transfer continues until the food's temperature evens out with its surroundings.

During the cooling process, foods release **moisture** as they cool. For example, bread releases **steam**. This can be seen as small water droplets on the surface of the baked item. This moisture release can affect the texture and can sometimes lead to items becoming slightly less crispy on the outside.

The Browning Magic

When you bake various foods, including bread, pastries, and meats, they undergo a chemical reaction known as the **Maillard reaction**. The Maillard reaction is responsible for the appealing colors, flavors, and aromas we associate with baked, grilled, or roasted foods. It occurs when proteins and sugars (such as glucose and fructose) in the food are exposed to heat. The reaction begins at temperatures around 300°F (150°C).

During the Maillard reaction, the amino acids (the building blocks of proteins) and the sugars interact in a series of complex chemical reactions. The initial reaction produces various compounds, including water, carbon dioxide, and nitrogen compounds. These compounds are essential for the creation of new flavors and aromas.

The Crumb Magic

The presence of tiny air bubbles primarily creates the crumb structure in baked foods. During baking, the heat causes the moisture in the dough or batter to turn into steam. This steam expands and forms pockets within the dough or batter. The gas from the leavening agents (like yeast or baking powder) also contributes to this expansion. These air bubbles are the building blocks of the crumb structure.

Gluten, a protein found in wheat flour, plays a crucial role in crumb structure. When flour is mixed with water, the proteins gliadin and glutenin combine to form gluten. This gluten network provides structure to the baked goods. In bread, for example, a well-developed gluten network results in a chewy and elastic crumb structure, while in cakes, a less developed gluten network leads to a tender and crumbly texture.

The choice of leavening agents (like yeast, baking powder, or baking soda) can significantly impact the crumb structure. Yeast produces carbon dioxide gas through fermentation, resulting in a crumb with small, irregularly spaced air pockets. Baking powder and baking soda produce carbon dioxide gas when they react with acids in the batter, leading to a finer and more regular crumb.

The time and temperature at which the baking occurs are critical factors. Longer baking times can lead to a drier crumb, while higher temperatures can quickly set the crumb structure.

(6) Homemade Marinated Grilled Chicken

Grill

Cooking marinated grilled chicken is like embarking on a delicious scientific adventure! When you marinate chicken, you're using the magic of science to transform simple ingredients into mouthwatering flavors. As you grill it, you're harnessing the power of heat and chemistry to create those tempting grill marks and caramelization. You'll learn about how different ingredients in the marinade work together and how heat can transform them into a delectable meal.

Ingredients

- 4 boneless, skinless chicken breasts
- 1/4 cup olive oil
- 1/4 cup soy sauce
- 1/4 cup lemon juice
- 2 cloves garlic, minced
- 1 teaspoon dried oregano
- 1 teaspoon paprika
- Salt and pepper

Equipment

- Grill (charcoal or gas)
- Ziplock bag or airtight container
- Tongs
- Meat thermometer

Instructions

(1) Prepare the marinade

Combine olive oil, soy sauce, lemon juice, minced garlic, dried oregano, paprika, salt, and pepper in a bowl to create your marinade. Stir well

(2) Marinate the chicken

Place the chicken breasts in a ziplock bag or airtight container and pour the marinade over them. Make sure the chicken is fully coated. Seal the bag or container and refrigerate for at least 30 minutes (or up to 24 hours for best flavor).

(3) Preheat the grill

Preheat your grill to medium-high heat. If you're using a charcoal grill, light the charcoal and let it burn until covered with white ash. For a gas grill, preheat to around 375-400°F (190-200°C).

(4) Prepare the chicken

Remove the marinated chicken from the bag or container and let any excess marinade drip off. Discard the remaining marinade.

(5) Grill the chicken

Place the chicken on the preheated grill. Grill each side for about 6-8 minutes, or until the internal temperature reaches 165°F (74°C). You can brush with extra marinade during grilling if desired.

(6) Rest the chicken

Remove the grilled chicken from the grill and let it rest for a few minutes. This allows the juices to redistribute and keeps the chicken tender.

(7) Serve and enjoy!

Slice the chicken and serve with your favorite side dishes like grilled vegetables or a salad.

The Marinated Science Behind the Grilled Chicken

Marinating Magic: When you mix ingredients like oil, acid (from vinegar or citrus), and herbs or spices, you create a flavorful mixture. The acid helps break down the chicken's proteins, making it tender and allowing the flavors to penetrate.

Taste Transformation: The marinade molecules seep into the chicken, altering its taste. This process turns plain chicken into something extraordinary.

Heat's Impact: When grilling the marinated chicken, you apply heat. Heat causes the chicken's proteins to change, turning from a soft, pale color to a delicious golden brown.

Caramelization: As the chicken sizzles on the grill, the sugars in the marinade caramelize, forming those delightful, crispy layers.

(7) Beef Kabobs Sizzling Discoveries

Grill

Imagine marinating pieces of beef with tasty seasonings and then threading them onto skewers. The heat transforms the meat as you cook the kabobs, making it tender and flavorful. You get to experiment with different marinade flavors in a fun way to explore your culinary creativity and satisfy your taste buds simultaneously. Enjoy your beef kabobs and the tasty science adventure!

Ingredients

- 1 pound (450g) of beef
- Bell peppers, onions, and cherry tomatoes
- Olive oil
- Lemon juice
- Minced garlic (2 cloves)
- Salt and pepper
- Your choice of spices (paprika, cumin, and oregano work well)

Equipment

- Grill (charcoal or gas)
- Mixing bowl
- Tongs
- Wooden skewers (soak them in water for 30 minutes)

Instructions

(1) Prepare the beef

Begin by cutting the beef into bite-sized pieces. If you're using wooden skewers, soak them in water to prevent burning on the grill.

(2) Prepare the marinade

In a mixing bowl, combine olive oil, lemon juice, minced garlic, salt, pepper, and your chosen spices.

(3) Marinate the beef

Place the beef pieces in the mixing bowl and pour the marinade over them. Make sure the beef is well-coated. Cover the bowl and refrigerate for at least 30 minutes. If you can, leave it overnight for a more intense flavor transformation.

(4) Preheat the grill

Preheat your grill to medium-high heat. You can also use a stovetop grill pan if you don't have an outdoor grill.

(5) Prepare the skewers

Thread the marinated beef, bell peppers, onions, and cherry tomatoes onto your soaked skewers. Experiment with different combinations for a colorful and delicious result.

(6) Grill the beef

Place the kabobs on the grill and cook for approximately 10-15 minutes, turning them occasionally. You'll know they're done when the beef is cooked to your preferred level (rare, medium, or well-done).

(7) Remove the skewers and enjoy

Carefully remove the skewers from the grill and let them cool for a moment. Take a bite and enjoy the taste!

The Marinated Science Behind the Grilled Beef Kabobs

Marination Magic: Before you start grilling, you marinate the beef. The acid in the marinade helps break down the hard fibres in the meat, making it tender and flavorful.

Heat Transformation: When you place the beef kabobs on the grill, heat from the fire or the grill's burners begins to penetrate the meat. This heat causes the proteins in the beef to change, a process called denaturation. The meat starts to brown on the outside, forming that tasty crust.

Flavorful Chemistry: As the beef cooks, the marinade flavors are absorbed, infusing the meat with delicious tastes. So not only does the heat transform the beef's texture, but it also carries the flavors from your marinade into the meat.

(8) Burger Science Adventure

Grill

Cooking a homemade burger is not just about creating a tasty meal but also a fun science experiment! When you make a burger, you're becoming a burger scientist. You can explore the magic of transforming raw meat into a delicious patty. When you build your burger masterpiece, you're not just cooking; you're doing delicious science, and it's a blast! Enjoy the tasty experiment!

Ingredients

- 1 pound (450g) ground beef
- 1/2 teaspoon salt
- 1/4 teaspoon black pepper
- 4 hamburger buns
- Toppings like lettuce, tomato, cheese, and condiments
- 1/2 cup (120ml) water

Equipment

- Grill or stovetop griddle
- Spatula
- Meat thermometer

Instructions

(1) Prepare the meat

Take the ground beef and gently shape it into a round patty about 1 inch thick. Sprinkle salt and pepper on both sides. This is where your burger's flavor begins to form.

(2) Heat it up

Place your patty on a preheated grill or griddle. The heat causes the meat's proteins and fats to react. This reaction not only cooks the patty but also creates those delicious flavors and grill marks.

(3) Flip the patty	**(4) Watch the temperature**
After a few minutes, use your spatula to carefully flip the patty. This flip helps the juices inside redistribute, keeping the meat moist and tasty.	To ensure your burger is safe to eat, you need to cook it to a specific temperature. Use a meat thermometer to check. The magic number is 160°F (71°C). At this temperature, any harmful bacteria in the meat are destroyed.
(5) Toast the bun	**(6) Assemble and enjoy**
While the patty is cooking, toast the bun. When you toast the bun, it makes your burger even tastier.	Once your burger reaches 160°F, it's time to assemble. Place your patty on the toasted bun and add your favorite toppings. Enjoy your delicious creation!

The Tasty Science Behind the Burger

Meat Transformation: When you start with ground beef, you deal with proteins and fats. As you cook the burger, these components go through some exciting changes. The heat causes the proteins to denature, unfolding from their original state.

Flavor Development: As the burger cooks, the Maillard reaction happens. It's not as complicated as it sounds – it's just a reaction between amino acids (from proteins) and reducing sugars. This reaction creates those beautiful brown grill marks and also adds a lot of flavor. That's why your burger tastes so good!

Juiciness: You know that juicy, mouthwatering feeling when you bite into a burger? It's all thanks to fat. The fat in the meat melts as it heats up, making the burger moist and flavorful. Juicy science at its finest!

(9) Grilled Corn on the Cob Smokey Science

Grill

Imagine a magical transformation when we place fresh corn on the grill. The heat from the grill starts to break down the complex sugars inside the corn kernels, turning them into golden, caramelized sweetness. As the corn cooks, we can see the changes in color and smell the mouthwatering aroma. By cooking this tasty snack, you're also exploring the science of heat, caramelization, and transformation – all while having a fantastic time!

Ingredients

- Fresh corn on the cob (as many as you need)
- Butter (1/2 cup)
- Salt (1 teaspoon)

Equipment

- Aluminum foil (for wrapping)
- Grilling equipment
- Large bucket

Instructions

(1) Prepare the corn

Peel back the husks, but don't remove them. Leave a few inner layers attached.

Remove the silk threads, those are the fine, hair-like things.

Pull the husks back up to cover the corn.

(2) Soak the corn

Fill a large bucket or your kitchen sink with water.

Soak the corn in the water for about 15-20 minutes. This helps prevent the husks from burning on the grill.

(3) Prepare the butter	(4) Wrap in foil
Melt the butter in a microwave or on the stove. Mix in the salt to create a tasty, seasoned butter.	Place each corn on a piece of aluminum foil. Brush the corn with the seasoned butter, ensuring it's well coated. Wrap the corn tightly in the foil, creating little foil packages.

(5) Grill the corn	(6) Unwrap and serve
Preheat your grill to medium-high heat (around 350-400°F or 175-200°C). Place the foil-wrapped corn on the grill grate. Close the grill and cook for 20-25 minutes, turning occasionally. The husks will get slightly charred, and the corn will become tender inside.	Carefully unwrap the foil, and let the corn cool for a minute. Now, you're ready to enjoy your sweet, smoky grilled corn on the cob!

The Smokey Science Behind the Grilled Corn on the Cob

Heat Transfer: The grill's heat source, typically charcoal or gas, transfers heat to the grates. When you place the corn on the grill, the heat is conducted from the grates to the corn's surface.

Caramelization: Corn is naturally sweet, thanks to the sugar content in the kernels. When exposed to high heat, the sugars undergo a process called caramelization. This is when they break down and turn brown, creating that mouthwatering sweetness and rich flavor.

Maillard Reaction: The Maillard reaction occurs when amino acids (from proteins) and reducing sugars (like glucose) react under high heat. This reaction results in the desirable color and flavor of the grilled corn.

Moisture Evaporation: As the corn cooks, the heat causes moisture to evaporate from the kernels. This loss of moisture concentrates the sugars, intensifying the corn's flavor.

(10) Grilled Quesadillas Dessert Discovery

Grill

Cooking grilled dessert quesadillas is not just delicious; it's also a fantastic science experiment. As you sizzle the quesadillas on the grill, the ingredients change and transform in exciting ways. You'll even explore concepts like heat transfer and chemical reactions while creating a mouthwatering treat. So, have fun experimenting and enjoy your dessert quesadillas!

Ingredients

- 4 flour tortillas
- 1/2 cup chocolate chips
- 1/2 cup sliced strawberries
- 1/4 cup marshmallows
- Cooking spray

Equipment

- Grill
- Spatula
- Plates
- Tongs

Instructions

(1) Prepare the grill

Preheat the grill to medium heat (around 350°F or 175°C). Make sure to have an adult's help with this step.

(2) Prepare the Quesadillas

Lay out one tortilla and sprinkle half of it with chocolate chips, sliced strawberries, and marshmallows. Fold the tortilla in half to cover the ingredients. It should look like a half-moon.

(3) Grill the quesadillas

Lightly spray the grill grates with cooking spray to prevent sticking. Place the filled tortillas on the grill. Grill for about 2-3 minutes on each side until they're crispy and the chocolate and marshmallows are melted. Use a spatula and tongs to flip them gently.

(4) Cool and enjoy

Carefully remove the quesadillas from the grill onto a plate. Let them cool for a minute as the filling can be very hot. Enjoy the taste of your grilled quesadillas dessert!

The Sweet Science Behind the Grilled Quesadillas

Heat Transfer: When you place your dessert quesadilla on the grill, you're using a cooking method called conduction. The grill grates get hot, and that heat is transferred to the quesadilla when it makes contact. This is similar to how you feel the warmth of a hot mug when you hold it.

Caramelization: As the quesadilla heats up, the sugars in the tortilla begin to caramelize. Caramelization is a chemical reaction when sugars break down into various compounds, giving the tortilla those brown spots and a sweet, toasted flavor.

Melting Chocolate and Marshmallows: The heat causes the chocolate and marshmallows inside the quesadilla to melt. Melting is a phase change from solid to liquid due to increased temperature. When these ingredients cool down, they solidify again, creating a gooey, chewy filling.

Grill Marks: The grill's grates leave those iconic grill marks on your quesadilla. This happens due to the Maillard reaction, another chemical process. It involves amino acids and reducing sugars reacting under heat to create those distinct grill lines and deepen the flavor.

Heat Conduction and Insulation: You'll learn about heat conduction and insulation as you manage the heat on the grill. Some areas of the grill get hotter than others, and you'll have to adjust your cooking technique to ensure your quesadilla is evenly cooked.

Science Unleashed

The Art Science of Grilling Food

Grilling food is a delicious way to prepare your favorite meals and a fascinating scientific process. From the sizzle of the meat on the grill to the incredible flavors you experience, it's all rooted in science. Grilling is a cooking method that uses an open flame, whether it's from charcoal, gas, or wood, to cook food. It combines heat transfer, chemical reactions, and a touch of physics.

Heat Transfer Art

When you light your grill, you create a source of heat. **Heat is a form of energy** that travels from the grill grates to your food through several mechanisms.

Conduction is the direct transfer of heat from one solid object to another through physical contact. When you place food on the grill grates, the heat from the grates is conducted to the food.

Convection: Convection is heat transfer through a fluid, like air. As the air in the grill gets hot, it rises, creating currents. These currents carry heat to the food.

Radiation: Radiation is the transfer of heat through electromagnetic waves. In a grill, the flames emit infrared radiation. This radiant heat penetrates the surface of the food and cooks it from the inside.

Maillard Reaction Art

Maillard is a complex **chemical reaction** between amino acids (the building blocks of proteins) and reducing sugars. It's responsible for grilled food's browning, flavor, and aroma. When you grill a steak or burger, the heat causes the surface of the meat to reach temperatures that trigger the **Maillard reaction**. This reaction creates hundreds of flavor compounds and gives the food its irresistible taste. It's the reason why grilled meats have that beautiful sear and deep, savory flavor.

Grill Marks Art

Have you ever noticed those perfect grill marks on your burger or chicken breast? Those are a result of the Maillard reaction, too. The grates of your grill are made of metal, and they get extremely hot. When the meat comes into direct contact with the hot metal, it causes the Maillard reaction to create those grill marks. These grill marks not only look appealing but also enhance the flavor.

Place the food diagonally on the grill grates to achieve perfect grill marks, let it cook for a while, then rotate it 90 degrees. This creates an aesthetically pleasing pattern while ensuring even cooking.

Caramelization Art

Another essential process is **caramelization**, responsible for those sweet, brown crusts you see on grilled items, like caramelized onions or the sear marks on a steak. Caramelization happens when sugars are exposed to high heat. They break down into different compounds, creating those delightful browning effects and a sweet, toasted flavor.

Cooking Time and Temperature Arts

Different foods require varying times and temperatures for grilling. This is because the structures and compositions of various foods react differently to heat. For instance:

Proteins: Meat, poultry, and seafood contain proteins that change when exposed to high heat. Heat causes these proteins to denature, coil, and bond with each other, leading to the firm texture and altered flavor of grilled items.

Starches: Starchy vegetables like potatoes or corn undergo gelatinization, the swelling and subsequent thickening of starch granules when heated. This gives them that creamy interior while maintaining a crisp exterior.

Moisture and Smoke Rings Art

Grilling meat also involves managing moisture levels. **Moisture** evaporates from the meat's surface and then **condenses** on the cooler surfaces further in. This moisture contains **volatile compounds** from the smoke. It creates a smoke ring—an area of pinkish meat, just under the surface, that's highly flavorful and indicative of well-grilled barbecue.

Smoking and Flavor Art

Smoking food during grilling is another dimension of flavor. It's about heat and the **flavorful compounds** burning wood chips or charcoal produces. The smoke imparts a smoky aroma and taste to the food.

Wood Types: Different types of wood create various flavors. For example, mesquite wood adds a robust and smoky flavor, while fruitwoods like apple or cherry provide a milder, sweeter smokiness.

Volatiles: When wood chips smolder or burn, they release volatile compounds. These compounds bind to food surfaces, enhancing their flavor.

(11) A Journey into Mac and Cheese Science

Boil

Cooking homemade mac and cheese is not just about creating a delicious meal; it's also an incredible science experiment! Imagine mixing pasta, creamy cheese sauce, and the magic of heat to transform simple ingredients into a mouthwatering dish. You get to explore the science of melting and learn how starch in pasta thickens the sauce. So, grab your apron, and let's embark on a culinary adventure filled with cheesy science!

Ingredients

- 2 cups elbow macaroni
- 4 cups water
- 2 cups shredded cheddar cheese
- 1/2 cup milk
- 1/4 cup butter
- 1/4 cup all-purpose flour
- 1/2 teaspoon salt
- 1/2 teaspoon black pepper
- 1/2 teaspoon paprika (optional)

Equipment

- Medium-sized pot
- Large saucepan
- Whisk
- Wooden spoon
- Colander
- Baking dish
- Oven (with adult supervision)

Instructions

(1) Boil the macaroni

Fill the medium-sized pot with water. Add the macaroni to the water.	Place the pot on the stove over medium-high heat. Allow the water to come to a boil.	Let the macaroni cook for about 8-10 minutes until it's soft but not mushy. Drain the cooked macaroni in a colander.

(2) Prepare the cheese sauce

In the large saucepan, melt the butter over medium heat. Stir in the flour and cook for about 1 minute until it turns a light golden color. Slowly whisk in the milk, and keep whisking until the mixture thickens. Add the shredded cheddar cheese and stir until it's smooth and creamy. Season the cheese sauce with salt, pepper, and paprika (if you want a little kick).

(3) Mix the macaroni and the cheese sauce

Combine the cooked macaroni and the cheese sauce in a baking dish. Gently stir until the macaroni is coated with the cheesy goodness.

(4) Bake the mac and cheese

Preheat the oven to 350°F (175°C) with adult supervision. Place the baking dish in the preheated oven. Bake for about 30 minutes until the top is golden and crispy. Remove from the oven and enjoy your mac and cheese!

The Cheesy Science Behind the Mac and Cheese

Boiling Macaroni: When you boil macaroni, you're using heat to make the starches in the pasta absorb water. This causes the macaroni to swell and soften, turning it from hard and crunchy to soft and delicious.

Making the Cheese Sauce: The butter and flour mixture is called a roux. It helps thicken the sauce. Milk contains proteins that unwind and bond together when heated, giving the sauce a creamy texture. The cheese contains fats and proteins that melt, creating a gooey, cheesy consistency.

Baking the Mac and Cheese: Baking helps to melt the cheese further and allows the top layer to become crispy and golden brown, adding a delightful contrast to the creamy macaroni and cheese underneath.

(12) Exploring Chicken Noodle Soup Science

When you mix ingredients like chicken, veggies, and noodles, you explore the fascinating world of chemistry and physics in your kitchen. You'll learn how heat transforms raw ingredients into a comforting meal and observe how liquids boil and condense. Plus, the science of flavor is at play as spices and ingredients interact to create a tasty broth. Enjoy both the meal and the knowledge!

Ingredients

- 2 boneless, skinless chicken breasts
- 8 cups of water
- 2 carrots, sliced
- 2 celery stalks, chopped
- 1 small onion, chopped
- 2 cloves of garlic, minced
- 1 bay leaf
- 1 teaspoon salt
- 1/2 teaspoon black pepper
- 2 cups egg noodles

Equipment

- Large pot
- Cutting board
- Knife
- Measuring cups and spoons
- Wooden spoon
- Thermometer

Instructions

(1) Boil water

Pour 8 cups of water into the pot. Place the pot on the stove. Turn on the heat to high.		Observe how the water starts to bubble and steam as it reaches its boiling point at 212°F (100°C).

(2) Add chicken

Carefully put the chicken breasts into the boiling water. Notice how the chicken changes color from pink to white as it cooks.

(3) Chop veggies

While the chicken is cooking, chop the carrots, celery, onion, and garlic. As for an adult help for this step! Discuss how cutting increases the surface area for better flavor extraction.

(4) Simmer

After 15 minutes, reduce the heat to medium-low. Simmering at lower temperatures keeps the flavors melding together. Add the chopped vegetables, bay leaf, salt, and pepper. Observe the simmering process.

(5) Shred the chicken

Use a thermometer to ensure the chicken is fully cooked, reaching an internal temperature of 165°F (73.9°C). Remove the cooked chicken breasts from the pot and place them on a cutting board. Use two forks to shred the chicken into small pieces.

(6) Cook the noodles

Add 2 cups of egg noodles to the soup. Notice how noodles absorb water and become tender. Stir everything together and continue simmering for another 5-10 minutes.

(7) Serve and enjoy!

Ladle your homemade chicken noodle soup into bowls.

Enjoy your delicious creation, and discuss the science behind making this comforting soup!

The Secret Science Behind the Chicken Noodle Soup

Heat Transfer: The first scientific concept involved is heat transfer. When you place your pot on the stove and turn on the heat, you use conduction to transfer heat from the burner to the pot. The pot then heats up and transfers that heat to the water inside.

Boiling Point: As the water heats up, it eventually reaches its boiling point, which is 212°F (100°C) at sea level. This is when the water turns into vapor (steam). The bubbles in the boiling water are pockets of steam rising to the surface.

Cooking the Chicken: When you add chicken pieces to the boiling water, the heat from the water is transferred to the chicken. This heat cooks the chicken by denaturing its proteins. This means the proteins change their structure due to the heat, becoming solid and turning from pink to white, indicating that the chicken is fully cooked and safe to eat.

Flavor Extraction: As the chicken cooks in boiling water, some of its flavors, as well as nutrients, are transferred into the broth. This gives the soup a delicious chicken flavor and provides essential nutrients.

Dissolving Solutes: When you add salt to the soup, it dissolves in the water. This is a process of solvation, where the water molecules surround the salt ions and pull them apart, allowing the salt to disappear into the liquid.

Starch Gelation: When you add noodles or pasta to the soup, these contain starch. The heat from the soup causes the starch molecules to absorb water, swell, and then leach out into the liquid. This thickens the soup in a process called gelation.

Vegetable Cooking: You add vegetables like carrots, celery, and onions to the soup. As the soup simmers, these vegetables are cooked through a process called diffusion. This is when the heat causes the water inside the vegetables to move from higher to lower concentration areas. This makes the vegetables soft and flavorful.

Emulsification: Tiny droplets form within the soup if you add a small amount of fat or butter. The soup's heat and motion help disperse these fat droplets evenly, creating a creamy texture.

Colligative Properties: The more salt you add to the soup, the higher the boiling point becomes. This is due to colligative properties, which change the properties of a solution. In this case, the boiling point increases as you add salt.

(13) A Whipped Mashed Potato Adventure

Boil

Cooking mashed potato is a hands-on journey where you can explore changes in texture and taste while learning the fascinating science behind turning ordinary spuds into the delicious food we all love. As you peel and boil the potatoes, you're witnessing the transformation of raw ingredients into something soft and delicious through the power of heat. So, grab your apron and prepare for a mashing adventure filled with scientific discoveries!

Ingredients

- 4 medium-sized potatoes
- 1/2 cup milk
- 4 tablespoons butter
- Salt to taste
- Pepper (optional)

Equipment

- Pot
- Masher
- Stove

Instructions

(1) Prepare the potatoes	(2) Cut the potatoes	(3) Boil the potatoes
Wash and peel the potatoes. This step ensures that any dirt or chemicals on the skin are removed.	Cut the peeled potatoes into small, even-sized chunks. Cutting the potatoes into even pieces ensures they cook at the same rate. Smaller pieces cook faster.	Place the potato chunks in a pot and add enough water to cover them. Boil the potatoes until they're soft and easily pierced with a fork (about 15-20 minutes).

(4) Drain the potatoes

Carefully pour out the hot water, leaving the potatoes in the pot. Draining removes excess water, preventing soggy potatoes.

(5) Mash the potatoes

Use a potato masher to crush the boiled potatoes. Mashing the potatoes ruptures their cell walls, releasing starch. Starch acts like glue to create a creamy texture.

(6) Add milk and butter

Add the milk and butter to the mashed potatoes. Mix until they are well combined. The fat in butter and the liquid in milk make the potatoes creamy. Mixing them disperses fats evenly.

(7) Season the mashed potatoes

Season your mashed potatoes with salt and pepper to taste. Seasoning enhances the taste, and the salt interacts with the starch to bring out the flavor.

(8) Serve and enjoy!

Your creamy mashed potatoes are ready to be served. Enjoy your homemade mashed potatoes and the science-filled journey of transforming raw ingredients into a delicious dish!

The Creamy Science Behind the Mashed Potato

Potato Structure: Potatoes are made up of starch granules and water. The starch granules absorb water and swell when you cook them, making the potatoes soft.

Boiling: When you boil the potatoes, you're applying heat. This heat makes the starch granules in the potatoes absorb water and swell up, causing the potatoes to soften and become easy to mash.

Mashing: When you mash the softened potatoes, you break the starch granules and cell walls, creating a smooth texture. This is why mashing is a crucial step in making creamy mashed potatoes.

Butter and Milk: Adding butter and milk enhances the flavor and creaminess of the mashed potatoes. The fats in butter coat the starch granules, making the mash smoother, while the milk adds moisture.

(14) Shrimp and Rice Pilaf Science Delight

Boil

When you combine the delicious flavors of shrimp and rice, you're making a tasty meal and exploring the science behind it. You'll learn how rice absorbs water, transforming raw shrimp into a mouthwatering dish, and how the right seasonings can enhance the flavors. You'll uncover the secrets of heat and timing in the kitchen as you cook, ensuring your shrimp and rice pilaf turns out perfectly.

Ingredients

- 1 cup long-grain white rice
- 2 cups chicken broth
- 1 pound large shrimp, peeled and deveined
- 1/4 cup butter
- 1/4 cup chopped onion
- 1/4 cup chopped bell pepper
- 2 cloves garlic, minced
- 1/4 cup fresh lemon juice
- 1 teaspoon lemon zest
- 1/2 teaspoon salt
- 1/4 teaspoon black pepper
- Fresh parsley for garnish

Equipment

- Measuring cups and spoons
- Large saucepan with a lid
- Skillet
- Wooden spoon
- Knife and cutting board
- Grater for lemon zest
- Lemon juicer
- Serving plates

Instructions

(1) Sauté Aromatics

In a large saucepan, melt the butter over medium heat. Add the chopped onion and bell pepper. Sauté for about 2-3 minutes until they become tender and fragrant.

(2) Add rice

Stir in the rice and cook for another 2-3 minutes. This step coats the rice with the melted butter and lightly toasts it.

(3) Pour Broth

Add the chicken broth to the saucepan. Stir and bring it to a gentle boil.

(4) Simmer

Once it's boiling, lower the heat, cover the saucepan with a lid, and simmer for about 15-20 minutes. Rice will absorb the broth and become fluffy.

(5) Cook shrimp

In a skillet, melt some butter over medium-high heat. Add shrimp and cook for about 2 minutes per side until they turn pink and opaque.

(6) Combine

In the last few minutes of cooking the rice, pour in the lemon juice and lemon zest. Stir gently to combine.

(7) Season

Season the rice with salt and black pepper. Adjust to your taste.

(8) Season and enjoy!

Place the cooked shrimp on top of the rice pilaf. Garnish with fresh parsley for a pop of color. Enjoy your shrimp and rice pilaf!

The Boiling Science Behind the Shrimp and Rice Pilaf

Heat Transfer: When you sauté the shrimp and rice in a hot pan, you're using heat to cause a series of transformations. Heat causes the shrimp to change color from translucent to pink and firm, denoting that they are cooked. For the rice, it helps to absorb the cooking liquid and expand while becoming tender.

Absorption: Rice is an excellent example of how foods absorb liquids. It's like a sponge; the rice grains take in the liquid as you add the broth. The starches in the rice gelatinize and form a creamy texture.

Chemical Changes: While cooking, the rice undergoes chemical changes due to liquid absorption, breaking down the starches and causing them to thicken the mixture. This is a process called gelatinization.

(15) Taffy Time: Maple Syrup Science Fun

Boil

Cooking homemade Maple Syrup Taffy is delicious and an exciting science experiment! When you heat maple syrup and allow it to cool, it transforms into a sweet, chewy treat. The science behind it involves understanding how heat changes the properties of the syrup. So, while you're enjoying your maple syrup taffy, you're also learning about the magical transformations that occur when you heat and cool ingredients. Plus, it's a sweet reward for your scientific curiosity!

Ingredients

- 1 cup pure maple syrup
- 1/2 teaspoon butter
- Clean snow or crushed ice
- Popsicle sticks or wooden skewers

Equipment

- Saucepan
- Small bowl of cold water

Instructions

(1) Prepare the snow or ice

collect clean, fresh snow in a clean tray or lay out crushed ice.

(2) Prepare the taffy mixture

In a saucepan, add 1 cup of pure maple syrup. Add 1/2 teaspoon of butter to the syrup. The butter adds a rich flavor to your taffy.

(3) Cook the taffy mixture

Heat the syrup and butter over medium-high heat. Use a candy thermometer to monitor the temperature. The goal is to reach 235-240°F (113-116°C). This is the "soft ball stage."

(4) Test the mixture

To check if the taffy mixture is ready, drop a small amount of the syrup into a bowl of cold water. If it forms a soft, pliable ball when submerged, it's ready.

(5) Pour the syrup

Carefully pour the hot syrup onto the clean snow or ice. Create small taffy strips by drizzling it over the cold surface.

(6) Roll the taffy

Let the syrup cool for a few seconds. Use a popsicle stick or wooden skewer to roll the syrup onto the stick. Roll quickly before it hardens.

(7) Serve and enjoy!

Your maple syrup taffy is ready to serve and enjoy!

The Sweet Science Behind the Maple Syrup Taffy

Heating Process: Maple syrup contains a lot of sugar dissolved in water. When you heat the syrup, as it reaches around 240-250 degrees Fahrenheit (115-121 degrees Celsius), the water in the syrup starts to evaporate. Evaporation is the process of turning a liquid into vapor (gas) when heated.

Concentration of Sugar: As the water evaporates, the sugar in the syrup becomes more concentrated. This means there's less water and more sugar. It's similar to when you dissolve sugar in water to make a sweet drink. As you heat the syrup, you remove the water, leaving the sweet, sugary part behind.

Cooling Process: When you drizzle the hot syrup onto the clean, packed snow, it cools down very quickly. As it cools, the concentrated sugar in the syrup forms a new structure. Think of it as sugar molecules coming together and arranging themselves differently.

Solidification: The rapid cooling of the snow turns the syrup into a solid again. The sugar molecules bond together, creating a chewy, taffy-like texture. This is an example of a physical change – it's still sugar but has gone from a liquid to a solid.

(16) Uncover the Secrets of Crunchy Chicken

Fry

Cooking homemade Fried Chicken is like embarking on a delicious scientific adventure! You'll learn how different ingredients work together to create the crispy, golden masterpiece you love to eat. You'll discover the magic of frying – how hot oil transforms the batter into that crispy coating. Plus, you'll see how the chicken's natural juices and the heat combine to make a mouthwatering meal. So, roll up your sleeves, put on your apron, and prepare to make the most delectable Fried Chicken!

Ingredients

- Chicken Pieces (e.g., drumsticks, thighs, or wings): 6-8 pieces
- Buttermilk: 2 cups
- All-Purpose Flour: 2 cups
- Salt: 2 tablespoons
- Black Pepper: 1 tablespoon
- Paprika: 1 tablespoon
- Garlic Powder: 1 tablespoon
- Cayenne Pepper (optional): 1/2 teaspoon
- Vegetable Oil: 4-6 cups (for frying)

Equipment

- Deep Fryer or Large Heavy Pot
- Food Thermometer
- Tongs
- Baking Sheet with Wire Rack
- Paper Towels

Instructions

(1) Brine the chicken

In a large bowl, place the chicken pieces and cover them with buttermilk. This helps make the chicken tender and flavorful. Leave it in the buttermilk for at least 30 minutes or even overnight in the fridge.

(2) Prepare the coating

In a separate large bowl, mix the flour, salt, black pepper, paprika, garlic powder, and cayenne pepper if you want a bit of heat.

(3) Heat the oil

In a deep fryer or large, heavy pot, heat the vegetable oil to 350°F (175°C). This is where the frying magic happens.

(4) Coat the chicken

Take each piece of chicken from the buttermilk, allowing any excess to drip off, and then coat it thoroughly with the seasoned flour mixture.

(5) Dip the chicken

Dip the chicken back into the buttermilk for a second coat.

(6) Double coat

Coat the chicken again with the seasoned flour mixture. This double coating ensures extra crispiness.

(7) Fry the chicken

Gently place each piece of chicken into the hot oil using tongs. Be careful; the oil is hot! Fry a few pieces at a time to avoid overcrowding.

(8) Check the temperature

Use a food thermometer to ensure the chicken reaches an internal temperature of 165°F (74°C). This is the safe temperature for cooked chicken.

(9) Drain

Remove the fried chicken pieces with tongs and place them on a baking sheet with a wire rack. This allows any excess oil to drain off and keeps the chicken crispy.

(10) Serve and enjoy

Your fried chicken is ready to enjoy! It's crispy on the outside and juicy on the inside.

The Crispy Science Behind the Fried Chicken

Batter Magic: The batter is like the chicken's armor. It's made from flour, spices, and a liquid like buttermilk or eggs. The science here is that the batter forms a protective layer around the chicken. When you fry it, the batter crisps up, sealing in the chicken's juices and flavors.

Maillard Reaction: The high heat triggers a chemical reaction called the Maillard reaction, which is responsible for browning the chicken's crust. This reaction is what makes the chicken look so delicious and taste amazing.

(17) Crispy Fries Lab: Double Fry Mystery

Cooking crispy fries is not just about making a tasty snack; it's also a fantastic science experiment. When you slice up the potatoes and drop them into oil, the high heat causes the water inside the potatoes to turn into steam, and this steam makes the fries puff up and become crispy on the outside. Plus, there's a secret science behind frying the fries twice. The first fry makes them soft on the inside, while the second fry turns them golden and super crispy. So, prepare to have a blast while cooking and discovering the science behind extra-crispy fries!

Fry

Ingredients

- 4 large russet potatoes
- 4 cups vegetable oil for frying
- 1 teaspoon salt
- 1 teaspoon paprika
- 1/2 teaspoon garlic powder
- 1/2 teaspoon onion powder

Equipment

- Sharp knife
- Cutting board
- Large bowl
- Large pot or deep fryer
- Slotted spoon
- Paper towels

Instructions

(1) Prepare the potatoes

Wash and peel the potatoes. Cut them into long, even strips, about 1/4-inch wide. Ask for an adult help for this step.

(2) Soak the potatoes

Soak the potato strips in a bowl of cold water for at least 30 minutes. Science Alert: Soaking helps remove excess starch, resulting in crispier fries.

(3) Prepare for frying

Heat the vegetable oil in a large pot or deep fryer to 325°F (160°C). The first fry at a lower temperature cooks the fries inside without making them too brown. Remove the soaked potato strips and pat them dry with paper towels.

(4) First fry

Gently place a handful of potato strips into the hot oil. Fry for about 3-4 minutes, until they are pale but cooked. Remove and drain on paper towels. Science Alert: The first fry is like par-cooking; it prepares the fries for the second fry.

(5) Second fry

Raise the oil temperature to 375°F (190°C). Fry the par-cooked potato strips for another 2-3 minutes until they're golden and crispy. Remove and drain. The second fry at a higher temperature creates the perfect crispy texture.

(6) Season and enjoy!

In a bowl, mix the salt, paprika, garlic powder, and onion powder. Toss the hot fries in this spice mix. Science Alert: Seasoning adds flavor and completes the delicious taste. Serve and enjoy the taste of your crispy fries!

The Crispy Science Behind the Extra Crispy Fries

First Fry: In the first round of frying, the potato fries get hot and absorb some oil. The heat also starts cooking the inside, making it soft and fluffy. This process removes some moisture from the fries.

Cooling Phase: After the first fry, you let the fries cool down. This is a crucial step. It gives time for the moisture inside the fries to turn into steam and escape. The outside might feel a bit leathery at this point.

Second Fry: In the second round, the fries return to the hot oil. Because most of the moisture has already escaped during the cooling phase, they puff up and turn golden and crispy on the outside.

(18) A Cheesy Journey into Mozzarella Sticks

Fry

When you cook Mozzarella Sticks, you learn about the magical transformation that happens when cheese goes from solid to gooey, and you'll master the art of creating crispy exteriors. The hot oil transforms the cheese into a delectable, golden treasure. Plus, you'll discover the power of temperature control and how it influences the texture of the cheese. So, get ready to explore the world of cheese and uncover the secrets of crispy, gooey Mozzarella Sticks!

Ingredients

- 12 mozzarella string cheese sticks
- 1 cup all-purpose flour
- 2 large eggs
- 2 cups breadcrumbs
- 1/2 cup grated Parmesan cheese
- 1 teaspoon garlic powder
- 1 teaspoon dried oregano
- 1 teaspoon dried basil
- Cooking oil (for frying)

Equipment

- Deep frying pan
- Tongs
- Baking sheet
- Cooling rack

Instructions

(1) Breading station setup

Set up a breading station with three shallow bowls. In the first bowl, place the flour. In the second bowl, whisk the eggs. In the third bowl, mix the breadcrumbs, grated Parmesan, garlic powder, dried oregano, and dried basil.

(2) Coat the mozzarella sticks

Take a mozzarella stick and coat it with flour, shaking off the excess. Then, dip it into the beaten eggs, allowing any excess to drip off. Finally, roll it in the breadcrumb mixture, pressing the breadcrumbs gently to adhere.

(3) Double coat (optional)

For an extra crispy coating, repeat the egg and breadcrumb coating process.

(4) Freeze the mozzarella sticks

Place the coated mozzarella sticks on a baking sheet lined with parchment paper. Make sure they aren't touching. Freeze them for at least 1-2 hours or until they are solid. This step prevents the cheese from oozing out during frying.

(5) Heat the oil

Fill your frying pan with about 2 inches of cooking oil. Heat it to around 350°F (175°C). You can check if the oil is ready by dropping a small breadcrumb into it. If it sizzles and floats, it's ready!

(6) Double coat (optional)

Carefully add the frozen mozzarella sticks to the hot oil using tongs. Be cautious to avoid overcrowding the pan. Fry for about 1-2 minutes or until they turn golden brown and crispy. Don't overcook; the mozzarella can melt.

(7) Freeze the mozzarella sticks

Using the tongs, take out the fried mozzarella sticks and place them on a cooling rack to drain any excess oil. The cheese will be hot and gooey, so be careful!

(8) Heat the oil

Serve your Mozzarella Sticks while they're still warm, you may use a side of marinara sauce for dipping. Enjoy the crunchy, cheesy magic!

The Cheesy Science Behind the Mozzarella Sticks

Melting Magic: Mozzarella cheese is unique because it melts beautifully. When you heat it, the cheese's fat molecules break apart and flow around, turning it into a gooey, stretchy liquid. The hot oil in your cooking experiment helps this transformation.

Coating Chemistry: To get that crispy coating on the outside, you'll dip the cheese sticks in a mixture of flour, eggs, and breadcrumbs. This creates a protective layer. When you fry them, the coating turns golden brown and crunchy due to a process called browning.

(19) The Hushpuppies Kitchen Lab

Fry

When you mix flour, cornmeal, and a few other ingredients and drop them into hot oil, you create a mini kitchen laboratory. The batter puffs up and turns into those golden, crispy balls. That transformation happens because of a process called frying. The outside gets crisp while the inside stays soft. So, cooking hushpuppies is like doing a delicious chemistry experiment right in your own kitchen, and the best part is you get to eat the results!

Ingredients

- 1 cup cornmeal
- 1/2 cup all-purpose flour
- 1 tsp baking powder
- 1/2 tsp salt
- 1/2 cup buttermilk
- 1/4 cup finely chopped onion
- 1 egg
- Vegetable oil for frying

Equipment

- Deep fryer or a large, deep skillet
- Mixing bowls
- Slotted spoon
- Paper towels

Instructions

(1) Prepare the dry ingredients	(2) Prepare the wet ingredients	(3) Combine dry and wet ingredients
In a mixing bowl, combine the cornmeal, all-purpose flour, baking powder, and salt. Stir until well-mixed.	In another bowl, beat the egg, then add the buttermilk and finely chopped onions. Mix them together.	Pour the wet mixture into the dry ingredients. Stir until everything is well combined. The batter should be thick but moist. It's essential not to overmix; a few lumps are okay.

(4) Heat the oil	(5) Form the Hushpuppies
Pour vegetable oil into a deep fryer or large skillet, about 2-3 inches deep. Heat it to 365-375°F (185-190°C).	Use a spoon or your hands to scoop up small portions of the batter. Drop these spoonfuls into the hot oil. They should sizzle and start to turn golden brown.
(6) Fry the Hushpuppies	(7) Drain, serve, and enjoy!
Fry each batch for about 2-4 minutes, turning the Hushpuppies occasionally, until they're golden brown on all sides. Use a slotted spoon to remove them.	Place the fried Hushpuppies on a plate lined with paper towels to drain excess oil. Serve them hot. Enjoy your yummy Hushpuppies!

The Crispy Science Behind the Hushpuppies

Leavening: The primary leavening agent in hushpuppies is baking powder. Baking powder contains both an acid and a base. These components interact when you mix the baking powder into the hushpuppy batter. The acid reacts with the base when exposed to moisture and heat, producing carbon dioxide gas bubbles. These gas bubbles get trapped in the dough, making it rise and become fluffy.

Frying: When you place hushpuppy batter into hot oil, several things happen:

- **Steam Formation**: The water in the batter turns into steam due to the high temperature of the oil. As the steam expands, it causes the hushpuppies to puff up and become light and airy.
- **Crispy Outer Layer**: The hot oil quickly seals the outside of the hushpuppies. This helps to prevent the oil from seeping into the batter and making them greasy. The batter cooks rapidly on the outside, creating a crispy crust.

(20) The Science of Fried Apple Pies

Fry

Mixing ingredients like flour, sugar, and apples is magical. The heat transforms these components, creating a crispy, golden crust while turning the apples into a gooey, sweet filling. You'll witness how heat changes the texture and color of your pie and how different ingredients work together to create a mouthwatering treat!

Ingredients

- 2 cups all-purpose flour
- 1/2 teaspoon salt
- 2/3 cup shortening
- 6-8 tablespoons cold water
- 2 cups apples, peeled, cored, and diced
- 1/2 cup sugar
- 1/2 teaspoon ground cinnamon
- 1/4 teaspoon nutmeg
- 1/4 cup water
- Vegetable oil for frying
- Confectioners' sugar for dusting

Equipment

- Mixing bowl
- Rolling pin
- Knife
- Cutting board
- Frying pan
- Slotted spoon
- Paper towels
- Plate
- Fork

Instructions

(1) Prepare the dough

In a mixing bowl, combine the flour and salt.	Cut in the shortening using a fork or pastry cutter until the mixture resembles coarse crumbs.	Gradually add cold water, one tablespoon at a time, until the dough comes together. Form it into a ball, then wrap it in plastic wrap. Chill in the refrigerator for at least 30 minutes.

(2) Prepare the apple filling

In a saucepan, combine the diced apples, sugar, ground cinnamon, nutmeg, and water. → Cook over medium heat, stirring occasionally until the apples are tender and the mixture thickens. This usually takes about 15-20 minutes. Remove from heat and let it cool.

(3) Roll out the dough

On a floured surface, roll out the chilled dough into a circle. → Use a knife to cut the dough into 5-6 inch circles. These will be your pie crusts.

(4) Fill and fold the pies

Place a spoonful of the apple filling in the center of each dough circle. → Fold the dough over to create a half-moon shape. Seal the edges by pressing with a fork.

(5) Fry the pies

Heat vegetable oil in a frying pan over medium-high heat until it reaches about 350°F (175°C). → Carefully add the pies, a few at a time. Fry until they turn golden brown, which usually takes about 2-3 minutes per side.

(6) Remove and serve the pies

Use a slotted spoon to remove the pies and place them on a plate lined with paper towels to drain excess oil. → Once they've cooled a bit, dust the pies with confectioners' sugar. Eat your delicious homemade fried apple pies!

The Crispy Science Behind the Hushpuppies

The dough rises due to the **leavening agent** (baking powder) and the heat from frying. This makes the pies light and fluffy.

Frying involves the **Maillard reaction**, which is responsible for the crust's golden-brown color and rich flavor.

As the pies fry, the **moisture** inside the apples turns into **steam**, creating a tender and sweet filling.

(21) The Sweet Secrets of Chocolate Fudge

Get ready for a mouthwatering adventure that's both delicious and educational! Discover how cocoa, sugar, and butter undergo remarkable transformations as you create a fudgy masterpiece. It's a hands-on experience that will satisfy your sweet tooth while teaching you the captivating science of crystallization and emulsification. Get ready to impress your friends and family with your newfound knowledge and your mouthwatering chocolate fudge!

Ingredients

- 2 cups (about 360g) semisweet chocolate chips
- 1 can (14 ounces) sweetened condensed milk
- 1/4 cup (60g) unsalted butter
- A pinch of salt
- 1 teaspoon vanilla extract

Equipment

- A medium-sized saucepan
- A wooden spoon
- An 8x8-inch square baking dish
- Parchment paper
- Measuring cups and spoons

Instructions

(1) Setup

Line the baking dish with parchment paper. This step is essential for easy removal of the fudge later.

(2) Combine ingredients

In the saucepan, combine the chocolate chips, sweetened condensed milk, butter, and a pinch of salt.

(3) Heat

Place the saucepan over low heat and stir constantly until the chocolate and butter melt. This melting process occurs because the heat is providing the energy needed for the solid chocolate and butter to turn into a liquid.

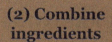

(4) Continue heating and stirring

Keep stirring the mixture until it's completely smooth. This step is where the sugar molecules in the condensed milk are dissolving in the chocolate mixture. We're also evaporating some of the liquid to make the fudge denser.

(5) Add vanilla

Remove the saucepan from the heat and stir in the vanilla extract. The vanilla adds flavor and aroma to our fudge.

(6) Pour into the dish

Pour the smooth mixture into the prepared baking dish. The mixture is still hot because it contains a lot of energy from the heat.

(7) Cool

Let the fudge cool at room temperature. As it cools, the sugar molecules in the mixture start forming a solid structure. This is the crucial step where our liquid fudge turns into a solid, yet creamy treat.

(8) Cut and enjoy!

Once the fudge is completely cool (which takes a few hours), lift it out of the dish using the parchment paper. Then, cut it into small squares or rectangles.

The Secret Science Behind the Chocolate Fudge

Melting: You start by melting chocolate and butter together. This is the first scientific secret! When you heat them, the chocolate and butter turn from solid to liquid. This change happens because heat gives the molecules in these substances more energy, making them move faster and become liquid.

Mixing: when you add sweetened condensed milk, you're dealing with emulsification. Emulsification means that the milk and chocolate mix together smoothly. You need to mix them well because liquids and solids don't usually get along, but you're making them cooperate!

Cooling: Once everything is mixed, you let the mixture cool. As it cools, the molecules slow down; this is where another scientific secret happens. Sugar crystals begin to form, which gives your fudge that fantastic texture.

(22) The Wobbly Science of Fruit Jellies

Have you ever wondered how those wobbly, colorful jellies you love are made? Well, it's not just magic; it's science! In this delicious experiment, you'll learn the secrets of transforming fruit juice into wobbly, chewy, and tasty jellies. We'll explore the role of gelling agents and the chemistry of flavor. Plus, you get to customize your own fruity flavors and shapes. It's a hands-on journey where your taste buds and curiosity will collide!

Ingredients

- 2 cups of fruit juice (e.g., apple, orange, or grape)
- 2 cups of granulated sugar
- 3 tablespoons of gelatin powder
- 1 cup of water

Equipment

- Measuring cups and spoons
- Mixing bowl
- Saucepan
- Whisk
- Silicone molds (in fun shapes)

Instructions

(1) Pick your fruit juice

Measure and pour 2 cups of your preferred fruit juice into a saucepan. Different juices bring different flavors and natural sugars.

(2) Add sugar

Add 2 cups of granulated sugar into the saucepan with your fruit juice. Sugar provides the sweetness we love in jellies. Stir to dissolve.

(3) Mix gelatin with water

In a separate bowl, mix 3 tablespoons of gelatin powder with 1 cup of water. Gelatin is like the secret ingredient that turns your liquid into wobbly jellies. Stir it well and let it sit for a minute.

(4) Heat and merge

Pour your gelatin mixture into the saucepan with the fruit juice and sugar. Heat the mixture gently while stirring. This helps to dissolve the sugar and gelatin.

(5) Cool

As your mixture cools, it begins its magical transformation into a jelly. The science at play is called gelation. It's like the superpower of turning liquids into solid gels.

(6) Mold

Pour your jelly mixture into silicone molds. Choose your favorite shapes; it's all about having fun! The jellies will take on these shapes as they set.

(7) Chill time

Place your molds in the refrigerator. This is where the real science happens. The cooling process allows the gelatin to set, turning your mixture into wobbly, chewy jellies.

(8) Unmold and enjoy!

Once your jellies are firm, carefully remove them from the molds. It's time to enjoy the fruity, wobbly treats you've created.

The Wobbly Science Behind the Fruit Jellies

Fruit Juice: The base of your jellies is fruit juice. Fruit juice contains natural sugars, which are essential for sweetness. Different juices have different types and amounts of sugar, impacting the flavor and sweetness of your jellies.

Sugar: Sugar makes your jellies sweet. When you mix sugar with fruit juice and heat it, the sugar dissolves into the liquid. This is a crucial step because it provides the sweetness and consistency you love in jellies.

Gelatin: When you mix gelatin with water and add it to your juice-sugar mixture, it transforms everything into a wobbly, jelly-like substance. This process is called "gelation."

Cooling: When you place your jelly mixture in the fridge to cool, the gelatin molecules connect, forming a network. This network traps the sugar, fruit juice, and water in a way that gives your jellies their fun, wobbly texture.

(23) The Candy Chemist of Lollipop

Desserts

Making homemade lollipops is a thrilling science experiment combining sugar, heat, and creativity to create your sweet masterpieces. With colorful flavors and shapes, you'll experiment with making your lollipops unique. Plus, exploring the chemistry behind how sugar crystals form as the syrup cools down will leave you amazed. With homemade lollipops, science has never been so sweet and satisfying!

Ingredients

- 2 cups granulated sugar
- 2/3 cup light corn syrup
- 3/4 cup water
- 1-2 teaspoons flavored extract (e.g., vanilla, cherry, etc.)
- Food coloring (optional)
- Cooking spray

Equipment

- Heavy-bottomed saucepan
- Candy thermometer
- Lollipop molds or silicone baking mats
- Lollipop sticks
- Oven mitts

Instructions

(1) Mix and heat	**(2) Add flavor and color**	**(3) Pour the mixture**
Combine sugar, corn syrup, and water in the saucepan. Insert the candy thermometer. Cook over medium heat without stirring until it reaches 300°F (150°C).	Remove from heat and add the flavored extract (and food coloring if desired). Stir well.	Carefully pour the syrup into lollipop molds or onto silicone mats. Place lollipop sticks into each mold.

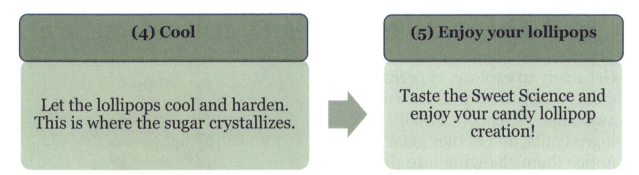

(4) Cool	**(5) Enjoy your lollipops**
Let the lollipops cool and harden. This is where the sugar crystallizes.	Taste the Sweet Science and enjoy your candy lollipop creation!

The Candy Science Behind the Lollipop

1. Sugar Crystallization:

Lollipops are made primarily of sugar. When you heat sugar, it goes through a process called **crystallization**. At high temperatures, sugar dissolves in water and becomes a clear syrup. But as it cools, the sugar molecules slow down and start forming solid structures, which are the sugar crystals. These tiny crystals stick together to give the lollipop its hard and shiny appearance. Temperature and the presence of other substances like corn syrup and water affect the speed of crystallization.

2. Temperature Control:

Temperature is a critical factor when making lollipops. The syrup needs to reach a certain temperature to achieve the right texture. As it cools, the sugar molecules arrange themselves into an organized structure. The final temperature determines whether you get a soft or hard lollipop. Higher temperatures lead to hard candy, while lower temperatures produce a chewy or smoother texture.

3. Flavor and Color:

You can add flavored extracts and food coloring to your lollipops. These elements don't just make the lollipop taste and look good; they're also part of the science. Flavoring is made from various compounds that give the lollipop its taste. Food coloring is often water-based and interacts with the sugar syrup to create vibrant colors.

4. Lollipop Stick:

Lollipop sticks are often made of materials that can withstand the high heat of the sugar syrup. These sticks help you hold the lollipop and add fun to your lollipop treat.

(24) The Strawberry Ice Cream Adventure

Get ready to explore, experiment, and create a tasty treat while learning some awesome science! You'll mix up ingredients, and as they get cold, you'll notice them changing into the creamy ice cream you love. Plus, you can customize your ice cream with toppings. Get ready to impress your friends and family with your newfound knowledge and your mouthwatering Strawberry Ice Cream!

Desserts

Ingredients

- 1 cup fresh strawberries
- 1/2 cup sugar
- 2 cups heavy cream
- 1 cup whole milk
- 1 teaspoon vanilla extract
- Ice
- Salt

Equipment

- Blender
- Mixing bowls
- Whisk
- Measuring cups and spoons
- Ziplock bags (1 quart-sized and 1 gallon-sized)

Instructions

(1) Wash the strawberries

Wash and hull (remove the green tops) the strawberries.	Cut the strawberries into small pieces. Put the strawberries into a ziplock bag and add 1/4 cup of sugar.	Seal the bag and gently smash the strawberries and sugar together. This will make a strawberry sauce.

(2) Prepare the ice cream base and mix the ingredients

In a mixing bowl, combine heavy cream, whole milk, and the remaining sugar. Add the vanilla extract and mix well.	Pour your sweet cream mixture into the quart-sized ziplock bag.	Also, pour the strawberry sauce from the previous step into the bag. Seal the bag, removing as much air as possible.

(3) Prepare for freezing and shake well

| In the gallon-sized ziplock bag, fill it halfway with ice and add about 1/2 cup of salt. | → | Place the quart-sized bag with the ice cream mixture into the larger bag filled with ice and salt. | → | Seal the larger bag and shake it gently for about 5-7 minutes. Make sure the ice surrounds the smaller bag. The mixture inside the smaller bag will gradually freeze and thicken. Keep shaking! |

(4) Scoop, serve, and enjoy!

| When the ice cream inside the small bag is thick, take it out. | → | Wipe the bag to remove any salt, then open it. | → | Serve your homemade strawberry ice cream in a bowl and enjoy! |

The Chill Science Behind the Homemade Ice Cream

Freezing Point Depression: You see, water usually freezes at 0 degrees Celsius (32 degrees Fahrenheit), but when you add salt to the ice, it lowers the freezing point. So, when mixed with salt, the ice can become much colder without turning into a solid block. This is why we use ice and salt in making ice cream.

Heat Transfer: Inside the small bag with your ice cream mixture, you have the ingredients like cream, milk, and sugar. These ingredients are a mix of water and fat. When you place this bag in the ice and salt mixture, heat from the ice cream mixture flows to the colder surroundings (the ice and salt bath). As the heat is removed from the ice cream mixture, the water content in the mix is frozen. The sugar and other ingredients in the ice cream prevent it from freezing solid like an ice cube. Instead, it turns into a creamy consistency.

Emulsion: An emulsion is when two liquids that don't usually mix well (like fat and water) are forced to stay together. Ice cream is an emulsion. In your mixture, the cream and milk fat forms tiny droplets dispersed throughout the water-based ingredients. This gives your ice cream a creamy texture.

(25) The Tropical Twist Smoothie Challenge

Creating your own Tropical Twist Smoothie is not just a delicious treat; it's a fantastic science experiment! You'll discover the secrets of blending different ingredients. Each component, from the frozen mango and pineapple chunks to the creamy Greek yogurt, uniquely creates the perfect taste. Adding honey and ice cubes allows you to experiment with sweetness and temperature. As you sip on your Tropical Twist Smoothie, you will explore the fascinating world of food science!

Desserts

Ingredients

- 1 cup frozen mango chunks
- 1/2 cup frozen pineapple chunks
- 1 ripe banana
- 1/2 cup Greek yogurt
- 1 cup orange juice
- 1 tablespoon honey (optional)
- Ice cubes (optional)

Equipment

- Blender
- Measuring cups and spoons
- Knife and cutting board

Instructions

(1) Tropical Prep

Place the frozen mango and pineapple chunks on the cutting board. With parental guidance, carefully cut them into smaller pieces, making it easier for the blender to work its magic.

(2) Banana Prep

Peel the ripe banana and break it into a few pieces. Toss them into the blender.

(3) Creamy Addition

Measure and add the Greek yogurt. This creamy ingredient will give your smoothie a delightful texture.

(4) Citrus Addition	(5) Sweet Addition	(6) Ice Addition
Pour in the orange juice. Notice how the liquid state of the orange juice contributes to the overall consistency of the smoothie.	If you like it sweet, add a tablespoon of honey. This step is optional, but it adds a natural sweetener to your creation.	Toss in a handful of ice cubes. Watch as the temperature of your smoothie drops, creating a refreshing chill.

(7) Blend the Smoothie	(8) Pour and Enjoy!
Secure the blender lid and blend everything together until smooth. Watch how the colors merge perfectly.	Pour your Tropical Smoothie into a glass. Enjoy the delightful taste of your homemade creation.

The Refreshing Science Behind the Tropical Smoothie

Tropical Ingredients: Mango, pineapple, banana, and citrus juice contribute more than flavors; they participate in scientific processes. Mango and pineapple are rich in enzymes like amylases, which help break down carbohydrates into simpler sugars. When you blend these fruits, these enzymes mix, causing a reaction that partially breaks down the carbs. This process begins the digestion of the fruit before you drink it, making it easier for your body to absorb the nutrients.

Banana's Texture: You notice a unique texture When peeling and breaking a banana into pieces—the soft, creamy interior and the bumpy exterior highlight the banana's cell structure. The internal creaminess consists of plant cells that are rich in starch. When blended, these cells break down, providing a smoother texture to your smoothie.

Greek Yogurt's Thickening Effect: The creamy Greek yogurt isn't just for taste. It's packed with proteins and fats. The fat in the yogurt helps stabilize the emulsion in the smoothie, creating a thicker texture. Moreover, proteins in the yogurt act as emulsifiers, stabilizing fat molecules with water-based elements like citrus juice, creating a well-blended mixture.

Future SmartMinds

www.futuresmartminds.com

Welcome to the **FutureSmartMinds** family!

Thank you for choosing "**Future Chef**" as your culinary adventure guide. We're thrilled to have you on board as we embark on a journey to develop the talents of young minds in STEM (Science, Technology, Engineering, and Mathematics) fields. Your support means the world to us. By investing in "**Future Chef**," you're not only inspiring young chefs but also empowering the future generation with invaluable STEM skills.

we kindly invite you to share your thoughts about "**Future Chef**" on Amazon. Your feedback helps us continue to improve and inspire more young minds. Your honest review will guide others in making their choice and encourage them to join us in shaping the future of our future smart minds.

Scan to Rate Us on Amazon

Once again, thank you for being a part of our FutureSmartMinds community. We're excited to have you with us on this journey.

Warm regards,

The **FutureSmartMinds** Team

www.futuresmartminds.com

Email: FutureSmartMindsKids@gmail.com

 @futuresmartminds

 @futuresmartminds

 @ futuresmartminds

Scan to visit our website

Please check our other kids' **STEM** activities books!

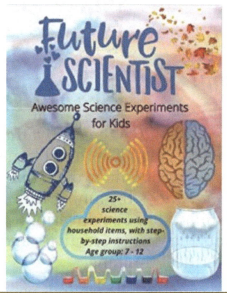

Available on Amazon!

Prepare for an exciting journey into the world of science! Our book is designed to captivate young minds, ages 7 to 12, with engaging experiments that uncover the magic of scientific concepts.

Unlock the World of Science: Science is all around us, and we've crafted mind-blowing experiments using everyday household items to demystify its wonders. These activities nurture analytical skills, critical thinking, and curiosity in physics, biology, chemistry, space, and technology.

Empowering Curious Minds: In a tech-rich world, kids yearn to understand how things work. These experiments unravel unpredictable phenomena, demonstrating that science explains the unexplained.

Hands-On Learning: Kids will hypothesize, experiment, understand, delve deeper into additional activities, and record their findings, fostering a lifelong love for scientific exploration.

What's Inside:
- 25+ Science Experiments on density, chemical reactions, soundwaves, brain functions, forces, heat transfer, Newton's laws, and rocket science.
- Mind-blowing Experiments like Musical Water Glasses, Rubber Band Guitar, Magic Milk, Dancing Flames, and Rockets!
- Science Explained with illustrations of core concepts and fun facts.
- Material Lists using common household supplies.
- Step-by-step Instructions, including illustrated graphics for safety.
- Science Behind the Experiment to understand concepts and results.

Grab your copy of "Future Scientist Awesome Science Experiments for Kids" and ignite the scientific spark in your child. Let the science adventures begin!

Available on Amazon!

Introduce your child to the captivating world of engineering." This exceptional book is tailored for budding young minds, ages 7 to 12, and is brimming with astonishing STEM engineering experiments that ignite creativity and critical thinking.

Unleash Engineering Wonders: Engineering is all around us, but sometimes it can seem complex. "Future Engineer" bridges this gap by unveiling mind-blowing engineering experiments that use everyday household items, making engineering accessible, exciting, and hands-on. These experiments spark curiosity and develop analytical skills.

Engineering: Where Imagination Meets Creation: As children in the age group of 7 to 12 grow, their curiosity knows no bounds. They are eager to unravel the mysteries of how things work. These fantastic experiments provide a hands-on tool to shape their interests and skills.

Hands-On Learning: Each experiment supported by easy-to-follow step-by-step instructions and material lists using items readily available at home. These experiments give young engineers the practical experience they need to grasp engineering concepts.

What's Inside:

- **25+ Engineering Experiments** on air pressure, Newton's laws of motion, heat transfer, surface tension, magnetism, windmills, and climate change.
- **Mind-Blowing Engineering Experiments** like an Air-powered Fast Car, a Screw Pump, an Air Cannon, a Nail Magnet, a Candle Carousel, and so much more!
- **Engineering Fun Facts**: Explore engineering concepts through colorful fun facts, such as Ancient Egyptian Technologies, Raindrops, Windmills, Sunlight, Climate Change, and Plastics.

Order your copy of "**Future Engineer Awesome Engineering Experiments for Kids**" and watch your child's fascination with engineering come to life. The future of innovation awaits!

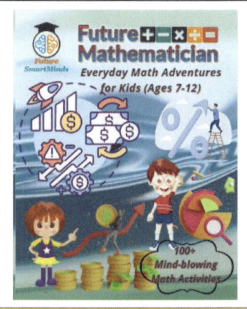

Available on Amazon!

Prepare your child for an exciting mathematical journey with "**Future Mathematician**." This extraordinary book is specially crafted for young minds, ages 7 to 12, making mathematics not just accessible but enjoyable, empowering them with the skills they need to tackle real-world math challenges.

Unlocking Mathematical Magic: Mathematics is everywhere around us, but sometimes it can seem disconnected from our daily lives. "**Future Mathematician**" breaks down these barriers, revealing the enchanting world of math that surrounds us every day. This book bridges the gap between the classroom and reality, showing kids the profound importance of math in their lives.

Interactive and Engaging: To make math an enjoyable adventure, each section of this book is accompanied by colorful, vibrant illustrations that convey complex mathematical concepts in an engaging and easy-to-understand manner.

Comprehensive Journey Through Math: "Future Mathematician" is not just another math textbook. It's a comprehensive guide that takes kids on a tour of various math topics, from the fundamental understanding of fractions and whole numbers to the exciting worlds of percentages, pie charts, budgeting, interest, investing, taxes, and number sense. It's a journey that covers the essential math skills kids need in their everyday lives.

Mental Workouts with Playful Characters: After each section, kids are invited to join fun characters in solving real-life math problems. These problems challenge kids to apply their newfound knowledge in practical situations, bringing math to life in a relatable and exciting way.

Grab your copy of "Future Mathematician" today and embark on a mathematical journey filled with discovery, fun, and empowerment.

Made in the USA
Las Vegas, NV
10 December 2023

82513932R00044